Acoustic Xpressions

poetry for the eclectic soul

Jacklyn Ireland

Copyright @ 2022 Jacklyn Ireland

ISBN: 978-1-7373670-1-7

All rights reserved.

No part of this publication may be reproduced, distributed, or transmitted in any form or by any means, including photocopying, recording, or other electronic or mechanical methods, without the prior written permission of the publisher, except in the case of brief quotations embodied in critical reviews and certain other noncommercial uses permitted by copyright law.

Cover illustration by Raphael (R.J.) Foster. Jacklyn Ireland's back cover photo credit: Glenwood Jackson; Jacklyn Ireland's MUA: Toni Walker

Dedication

To my daughter, Tanésha Davis, who was on my case about publishing my poetry, and friends whose names I dare not list for fear I'd forget someone who encouraged my writings.

And to my mother and father, Dorothy Horne and Robert Horne, who gave me life and introduced me to God, love of family, music, and reading at an early age.

Always, rejoicing in the Lord!

Drumroll Pleeze...

There are many kinds of poems contained in this collection.

Each section touches on the taboos of life, the beauty of nature, God's voice of assurance, human frailties and kindness, love, jazz, and the arts.

I hope these poems remind you of what it means to be alive.

Jacklyn Ireland

Your Guide to Enjoyment!

- **Part 1:** Life
- **Part 2:** Love
- **Part 3:** God Said
- **Part 4:** Nature
- **Part 5:** Music and Art
- **Acknowledgments**
- **About the Author**

LIFE

Broken Yet Peaceful

I lay in the blood of my son, he was a good man

Life gone, full of hope, and love taken while he honored God

I lay in the blood of my son; loving God is what he did. No hate only love

He shared Jackie Robinson's motto, "A life is not important unless it makes an impact on others."

My dress is soaked with the blood of my son

He tried to talk down a murderer confused by hate for people of a different race

I lay in the blood of my son

Dress, blood-soaked, my tears washing my face

He made others smile; now lying dead because of hate

I lay in the blood of my son, heartbroken and confused

He was a good man, protector of others, and abound in good deeds

Blood gives life and his now soaks my dress

He was life extraordinaire

I lie still with my dress soaked in his blood

Martin Luther King, Viola Liuzzo, Emmett Till, Mahatma Gandhi, Medgar Evers, and many more

I am a mother whose dress is covered with her son's blood

I remain strong, hopeful, and a peacemaker so the loss of my son is not in vain

The Horseman

It was as if I had known him a lifetime. He is the Horseman

Long legs slim and strong in character

He is the Horseman

Open to listen to others with plenty to share

Honored by royalty for his craft but humble before His God and never arrogant, he is the Horseman

Music bellows from his inner core celebrating a life of giving to those who could become lost in the wrongs of this world

He leads in the way of the Horseman – noble and wise

Connecting with God's creations, preserving earth, caring, and teaching us

The Horseman knows that life is a privilege and gift. He knows God has given each human person assignments for the common good of all

We must prevail

Sturdy and focused as he rides, he and horse become one heartbeat - one

All around, trees, birds, sky, earth, lakes, and streams join in one song to God as hoofs of the Horseman's stallion beat out a special rhythm

He is the Horseman, hearing what is special to his ears only - the beat of love, compassion, joy, wisdom, and peace cry loudly deep within and explodes to touch those in his path.

This is the mission of the Horseman. No fear – Protect!

Inspired by the work of Jean Albert Renault working with youth in Baltimore. Poem is featured in "Journey of a Horseman" documentary on the life of Jean Albert. (Produced by C&B Productions.)

Gallant One

Denying self, we know you by example, gallant soldier

Sensitive and loving, you finesse our hearts

Protector of country and family, we know your love touches us, chivalrous

Your presence assures us, as a defender of mankind

You speak truth and symbolize patience for what is good, attentive

Stunning in stature, defending what is right, courageously

Discipline and obligation to country are inscribed in your character

Working to make life beautiful for others, it is your call; we understand, our lives are blessed

Sworn to serve and save in times of war or peace, you protect

Weapons of warfare only supplement your gallantry and sacrifice; one can only imagine what you endure when no one's looking

Gallant one, the trail of service you leave strengthens us all

You serve with honor and endure the scars of battle

We pay tribute; however, it is not enough for your brave sacrifices

Good Results

Life is full of good results

Love brings joy

Kindness gives us cheerfulness

Worries have solutions

Despair becomes hope

Neglect brings attention

Tolerance brings understanding

Diversity clears misconception

Clarity triggers more thought

Knowledge brings understanding

Imagination sparks discovery

Life brings us happiness

Surprises change our expressions

Starting ignites a beginning

Passion stimulates creativity

Little acts of kindness exhibit thoughtfulness

An ending is another's beginning

A full circle of good results

Lonely

I am a lonely woman

> … who comes alive at your touch. It is magical. And dies like a puppet on a marionette's string when hands that manipulate it cease to move

I am a lonely woman

> … who sings of love when the thought of you sends rhythmic pulses that touches my very soul

I am a lonely woman

> …who knows true love, the feel of a held hand, a voice of assurance, sweet hellos, a glance that warms, a song whose melody never stops, a remembered kiss.

I am a lonely woman

> … who knows love and waits with anticipation

Old Hands

Old hands unite us with each touch, they have a solid message of love

They send out claps of joy on things we take for granted

Healing power generates from old hands with each soothing rub

Old hands have nourished many as they stirred pots of delicious meals

Old hands ease an itch and tend a wound

Quiets a room with a sturdy clap!

Pats the stranger to insure everything will be alright

Old hands have welcomed and sent many on their way

They are a symbol of wisdom, time tested, can't be replaced, and constructed to love

Old hands raise and acknowledge God's Word

And come together to pray for us

Beautiful
    Old
        Hands

I Am Human

Homeless — Don't look down on me, you don't know where I've been and the road I've traveled

Look into the face of the homeless! I am you!

Don't look down on me, I've traveled a hard road My heart beats the music of joy and sadness

And love reigns in and out of my life drifting to parts unknown

Hanging by a thread of homelessness and hunger, I indulge in habits and needs on lonely avenues, faceless to many

I venture up and down streets for customers, how did I get here?

Looks of disdain fill my life—it has been a while since I was touched

Words of kindness start healing of unspeakable troubles

Come closer

Smiles transmit caring

Thank you for your touch, magnifying humanity

I…Am…Human

Girl to Womanhood

Daughter, with love you were created

With pain you entered, and love was regained

You carry the banner of truth; it is your mantra and a spirit of discernment surrounds you

Precious one, your ways make you unique.

Ceaseless love – persistence - knowledge and loyalty

Compassion you know, and forgiveness is easy

Your beauty turns heads

A selfless, steady beat for justice radiates from your heart

Confidence moves with every step because you know you belong to God

Precious one, you seek advice and knowledge

The "know-it-all spirit" floats past and has no place in your life

Not easily fooled, patient for the truth—no time for games

Cute as a girl, beautiful as a woman—strong and observant

God leads your life

You are the love of so many lives

Pain brought you in and love pushes you forward

Daughter of dreams, supported by your ancestors—strong

Precious as a girl and now as a woman, sharing what you have learned from many who crossed your path

Lead

This is dedicated to my dear, sweet daughter, Tanésha, who I love beyond measure!

I Am Worthy

I am a woman composed of voluptuous hips, thighs and soft breasts that please the eyes of men

My walk unintentionally distracts and eyes follow

I am a woman

Eyes of brown, green, blue, and gray hypnotize and tell of unspoken truths that only mama knows

I am a woman composed of voluptuous hips, sturdy thighs and soft breasts

God's beauty

My crown is bald, curly, tight, permed, colored, gray, a creative beauty of God, He smiles. I am a woman, make no mistake

I am the cornerstone and with joy I serve, nurture, encourage and educate; I celebrate my calling

Beauty, wisdom, love, compassion, confidence, creativity – I am a woman composed of voluptuous hips, sturdy thighs and soft breasts.

Respect me

I am worthy

I am God's creation

Peace Call

In our world, many great and wonderful occurrences take place; however, we sometimes struggle for peace

We need peace
No more double shootings

We need peace
No more politicking

We need peace
No more looking the other way

We need peace with healing

We need peace
Initiatives to increase self-esteem, not an arsenal of guns

We need peace
To end the cries of mothers and fathers

We need peace
To allow kids to play freely

We need peace
To stop hearts from breaking

We need peace
Not a lot of media babble creating discourse

Peace is the path to sanity

Don't Be Fooled

The world is falling apart. Really? Said who?

It is under God's control

Memories are not getting lost; the pass-through is just a little smaller

Open up and share God's truths

Laughter is not dwindling; it slowed down just a little

We got to stir in the joy of the Lord a little bit more and depend on Him

When it's added, you will hear it. Just listen

It's waiting for you to remember God's joy and grace

Discard pessimistic thoughts

Love has not disappeared; we carry in our hearts memories of loved ones lost and gone; their imprint remains in our lives, like footprints left behind in dirt and sand

You will find trouble in the world but never lose heart or give up

Throw negativity to the wind; bury it and drop it, give God a chance

He conquered the world, find peace in Him

Take Note: Strength

Beautiful black and brown men constantly faced with challenges, how strong and stately you are

Statues of God's perfection faced with overwhelming odds, injustices, and those not taking time to listen. (**Note**: there are those who do hear you)

You are brave, forthright and magnificent with that special distinctive swagger you've been blessed with by nature. (**Note**: We see you even when you think we aren't looking)

You are sons of praying mothers and fathers, husbands of loving wives, caring fathers, comforters to many, and builders of communities. (**Note**: Let no one steal your cornerstone)

Make no mistake! You have a righteous destiny and historical roots that leave trails of wisdom, engineering feats, successes, and love. (**Note**: History speaks for itself, no matter how they try to hide it)

Outside Noise

What are you doing? Who told you that was possible?
    Outside noise, keep moving forward

You smile too much, no one will take you seriously
    Outside noise, keep smiling

Great writer, really? You can't put two words together
    Outside noise, keep writing

Don't listen to the outside noise whose goal is to defeat you
    Defeat **IT!!**

Voting is not your right
    Outside noise, cast your ballot

Education you are not entitled
    Outside noise, take advantage, study, and excel

Changing your mind again?

    Outside noise, keep being creative
Can't learn
    Outside noise, all things are possible, keep
    working at it

Sinner, God don't listen to you!
    Outside noise, rebuke the notion He doesn't
        Yes he does

Outside noise can confuse and hinder lives, if minus discernment
    Where is your outside noise coming from?

Is God involved?

LOVE

Whispers of Love

Do you hear it, whispers of love?

Like the wind, it brushes your face and kisses you lightly

Do you hear it, whispers of love, unmarked by apprehension, excited by romance?

Whispers spreading joy unselfishly

Do you hear it, whispers of love, breaking through to those without hope?

Touching the lonely, drying tears, offering peace, whispers of love carry like the wind to all in its path and the key to it is you!

Love Whisperer

Beautiful Black Man Justice

Justice is a Beautiful Black Man strutting with shoulders swaying, thick lips moving and the words, *"Hey baby"* being whispered, with his woman receiving those words with a deep sultry reply, *"Yes baby"*

The touch of his hands, feeling the softness of his lips and the wishes of onlookers craving for the same…

That's justice

He is backed by his woman when the world is trying to break him and she whispers, "You can do it"

Most of all, a portrait of integrity is the caring, noble, bold, innovative Black Man moving forward without fear, powered by the strength of his ancestors, family and friends…

That's justice, my Beautiful Black Man!

Swagger

His swagger moves her. It distinguishes him as the king he is born to be Dark and mysterious to those who see him warm and compassionate to her-- ***she knows him***

His tongue delights every part of her body -- ***it is their secret***

Thoughts of his visits linger and ignite her inner thighs -- ***he pleases***

Her ancestors cry out, NO! STOP! Instead…***she takes him again***

The whole world opens up and seeds of their ancestors meet -- ***passion***

They confirm emotions and lust, they have with no inhibitions -- ***they rest***

He swaggers out to confirm his marriage and his ancestors roar because that is where he belongs, not with the lover that steals his seed

He smiles as he leaves -- she contemplates his next visit

This is their secret affair -- dark and mysterious opposites

And one day…

                              he might stay…forever

If I Could

If I could pass it on to you

>…You would smile at the sound of your own voice, if only for a moment

>…You would know how happy I feel each minute we have together

>…Appreciate the simple, uncomplicated things about you that make me smile

If I could pass it on to you

>…You would feel what I carry each day for you and how pleasant it is

If I could pass it on to you

>…You would know my anticipation when you say *I'm on my way* and the let down *when you can't show up*

If I could pass it on to you

…You would know what a treasure you are to me
or maybe you already know, and there is no
passing on necessary

They Meet

I can't stay long, I know, but you came

I can't stay long, but you are so beautiful

I can't stay long, I know, but the softness of your lips soothes the soul

I can't stay long, I know, but your touch liquidizes every part of my body

I can't stay long, I know, but every ounce of passion within explodes when you are around

I can't stay long, I know, but just your presence alone rejects loneliness

I can't stay long, I know, but you came and my anxiety leaves

I can't stay long, I know, this one last kiss must linger until you return

You can't stay long, I know and understand, you must exit until next time

The memories remain and loneliness trickles in; it's just every now and then… love

Better known as a "night call"

Don't Live in Lost Love

My heart is broken because of lost love

Tears run like a rainstorm, but I refuse to stay there

Warm touches that set me on fire are doused by words of breaking ties

Lips that kissed with honey delivered a sting of truth

> …and a touch that rejuvenated was ceased, missed, and longed for; however, I refused to stay there

Time spent in the arms of a lover, no more

Embracing a new love

ME.

That Hat

Turn that hat around, let me see that face

Eyes brown with the light of the world shining through

A nose inherited from the tribe of your ancestors -- distinguished -- prominent -- proud

Lips thick, soft and luscious, each kiss electrifying

Turn that hat around, let me see that face

Smooth, handsome, chocolate, brown or vanilla

You move me

It's your world

Is there room for one more?

Sweet Chocolate Love

Sweet chocolate, don't you just love it?

If not, that's okay, it has plenty of fans

It comes from special plants that dance as they grow, I'm told

I don't know, but I love my sweet chocolate

Sweet chocolate makes my taste buds dance the tango, rumba and twist a little

Oh, chocolate, don't you just love it?

A few bites postpone disappointments and is the answer to lost love

Sweet chocolate has friends: nuts, caramel, and more

When they show up, the party commences

Oh, chocolate, don't you just love it?

Smiles appear and frowns disappear and along comes chatter joining in, too

Oh, chocolate, what's not to love?

He Knew

He kissed her and he knew

Holding her hand, he knew with each smile

Integrity is what she saw, but he knew

Her eyes saw only the beauty of this world, but he knew

Lost in the bliss of lovemaking, he forgot, but then he remembered

Never a cross word passed their lips, but he knew

Trusting God was her strength and giving of herself he admired, but he knew

Her beauty radiates in his eyes and a quick glance his way lets him know she cares, but he knew

She doesn't judge him for what he possesses, only his moral character, which he knew

He is a man and wants to give more but life's struggles overpowered him, and he knew it was time to disconnect.

She deserved more, he knew

A tear, one last hug, and the touch of her sweet lips, he turns and walks away

She knew he was a man of integrity; she wept

He didn't know

Fallen Tears

Each drop carries a story from the heart as they dance down faces

Stories of love extraordinaire, hearts connecting and dancing to sweet rhythm

Joy deep from within streaming outwardly accompanied by handclaps and words that overwhelm

Bondage broken and joined by tears of elation, drenching the face in a celebratory outpouring of joy and inter-cleansing

Each drop is significant

What stories do your tears carry?

A drop for compassion, good and bad times, memories lost?

Or healing tears coming from sharing a good cry?

Each drop carries a story kept in hearts

GOD SAID

Dimensions

Dimensions of oneness and unity improves life

Your victory lap celebrates

Peace determines life

God's salvation gives victory, grace, and saves us

Empathy shows understanding of God's message
Praying fights battles

Pain delivers anguish, it's real. God delivers relief

Spiritual birth connects us with God

Faith walks us through

Afraid a little? Just remember who your Father is; He never leaves you

Every moment in our life is an opportunity to honor God using your gifts and talents to change lives, revealing Him

We straighten hanging pictures for the sake of aesthetics; God straightens lives to give everlasting life

What dimension of life are you in?

Kin

Music unites us, our God fathers us. We share the sun, moon, and stars and gravitate to love in others

We are kin.

Thirsting for peace along the way we sometimes encounter misunderstanding; nevertheless, conversation helps us see sides

We are kin.

Feelings are deep, intense, and bold as we search for our place in the universe. We encourage

We are kin.

Kindness flows and humbleness streams in both directions; we are humankind and at the same, unique

We are kin.

Each of us are sculptured works of God, naked, then being filled by every accomplishment, gift, and bits of love we offer

We are all living proof that love is in the world through our existence

We are kin.

Unique

You are the most beautiful person in the room;
I know because God said so!

Created by unique and divine hands, your face is like no other -- eyes, nose, mouth, and cheeks stand out; you are His work of art. Stand tall as you enter the room

You are the most beautiful person in the room, let your uniqueness speak and celebrate God's handiwork

Be confident, don't shrink back, you have your own personal ID -- share it

No doubts, chill out, the world needs to experience your gifts to push forth God's authentic truth, given to you with His stamp of approval over you

Believe you are the most beautiful person in the room; you are a masterpiece

God said so!

Miracle

A miracle defying scientific law

Walk proudly and sprinkle your gifts with love and peace

You are God's creation with abilities to cultivate, encourage, spread knowledge, and love

It illuminates from every pore

You are a miracle in the making

Each day your eyes open, opportunities to share your gifts blossom

Touch, smile, declare, and carry them forth

You are a miracle in the making

Believe and see it -- softly caress it proudly -- display it -- live your purpose

You are part of a world that is turning, learning, and evolving

Get on, make your mark, illuminate your gifts in ways big and small

You are the miracle -- God's promise -- walking in His grace and mercy

Miracle child -- lift someone up

Disappointments Have No Place

Disappointments fly south and sometimes come back

Let them stay south and not overshadow the light of joy

Disappointments are sneaky little things out to shift the good in the atmosphere

Make them public and kick them out

We know who they are; don't let them stay around

Treat them like petals falling from a dying blossom, dead and gone

Designed to depress, they have no permanent place

They just wander, wishing to destroy happiness

Powerless to destroy unless you invite them in

Disappointments have a temporary life span

TRUST GOD!

Mask

Masked feelings speak no truth

Masked feelings lose out on the beauty of life

Masked feelings fade hope like falling tulip petals and bring rivers of tears because of unspoken words

Masked feelings stifle music of the soul, the pathway to creativity, and opens a hole in the heart that's never filled

Masked feelings are not part of God's plan. He spoke truth

Unmask

Let it flow

Don't lament

Connect and Live!

NATURE

Gardener Extraordinaire

God's work through you in your garden delights us all

It is like a sweet kiss as we eye brilliant colors and pleasant burst of fragrances only nature can create, through the Gardener Extraordinaire

Roses of many colors symbolize appreciation, love, gratitude, new starts, spirituality, and enthusiasm

No wonder we admire their beauty

Your lovely lilies dance with gaiety and passion in colors of orange and yellow, while sweetness and purity of heart peeks through each Lily of the Valley; they captivate and allure

God guides the hands of the Gardener Extraordinaire that gracefully enhances the garden's beauty as only He can

Soil filters through each hand, mixed with stone, dirt and clay permeating the smell of freshness

It is ready to feed and nurture as each hand manipulates the earth gently, placing it in its resting place in preparation to give and sustain life

Gardener Extraordinaire, your arrangements of love cause us to take a deep breath and connect with God's beauty, giving us life

Moon

Nightly, the sunlight bounces off your body and lights up your dull outer shell, fooling and mesmerizing us, no matter where we stand in the world

Mystifying us, though you've been touched and walked upon, we know not all you possess

Your lunar body keeps us grounded, however, voyages of emotional journeys materialize as words and music from the heart streams forth

Hovering above, easy to spot, in perfect peace, then disappearing like lost love

Bewildering, powerful, but slow moving, it drifts around like a nomad with no permanent home, going through phases—changing

Each sunset, the curtain opens, and your astronomical body makes an entrance, illuminating only what you choose to expose to earthly gazers

Igniting celebrations of renewal, spirituality for some, you light the sky and bodies of water dance -- beauty and intense luminance keeps us company

We are locked to your light

Fisherwoman

The fisherwoman knows her place by the lake; quiet and secluded, she's been there many times

Low sunlight on the lake, spotlight insects dancing over the water

Mesmerized by its beauty, the fisherwoman knows, eventually, something will take the bait

Quietly, she sits surrounded by trees and greenery remembering sunrises and sunsets of those who once joined her. She reminisces

The fisherwoman holds her pole steady; too much movement will stir the water, she knows calmness

God's music of the forest is all around her

Birds circle the lake then join her; a woodpecker hammers away and forest life joins in the chorus. Nature serenades the fisherwoman

She watches the lake waiting patiently,
not overzealous

Not moving or stirring, the fisherwoman knows in time what she has come for will happen

In the world of the fisherwoman, no hustle and bustle exist. No warring with schedules, she relishes peace and the first bite

Silence is broken; at first bite, the fisherwoman speaks only then, words to her prey

A fisherwoman's insights take us closer to what is real and before us

Patience is an art

Take time

This poem is dedicated to my mother, Dorothy Horne, who loved to fish while teaching her grandchildren fishing techniques using a bamboo pole.

Windowsills

Windowsills filled with plants flourishing and some barely holding on

Symbolic of life's journey, as we hold on, catching each petal of love, joy, sadness, and peace that falls upon us

Pots with little scratches of wear and tear are repurposed to hold close their contents on the windowsill. We must reimagine and fix challenges of this life and unlock our purpose -- it is at the very core of our existence

Tiny, winged creatures fluttering on the windowsill find life in plants, sucking the sap, weakening growth; withered and unhealthy, the beautiful glow is lost, imitating life's struggles and giving up

Don't be dissuaded. The phenomenal glow will return with a smile; kind words and acts and the light of hope and peace God gives will be an everlasting glow.

Sweep away those things that bug you, don't let them win

In each pot on the windowsill, roots pull from the soil nourishment needed for each leaf, stem or flower. We must anchor in place and strengthen our families, so our ancestral history and wisdom blooms and our roots maintain life

Like the roots and dirt of the plants, you are the foundation that feeds knowledge, love, peace, and hope. Your roots are strong so they can only flourish and bloom

Watering each plant sustains its beauty. The beauty of God's Word sustains us and spreads the beauty of His love

Sunshine hitting the windowsill enhances the life of each plant. We must be a ray of sunshine, lifting up and encouraging others, and nurturing our minds with positive energy

So, we flourish like plants on the windowsill and not cease to exist

MUSIC AND ART

Jazz

Hips sway as the trumpet plays, arms wave in the air to witness sounds that rejuvenate those memories of youth

Sweet, is the cry! The music is so intense. Trumpet virtuoso lets the audience have it, over and over, there is pleasure in the music. Oh yeah!

Jazz, the eager revolutionary, no barriers, hot and smooth. Voices raise to witness the bass player -- saxophonist -- drummer -- pianist as the groove fills the air with harmonic complexities that make you scream and yell, yeah!

Jazz / Sounds / Notes / Beats / Melodies make deep love and the drums of our ancestors come forth and explode   It permeates every pore

A lingering gaze, a kiss, a true promise, natural beauty, true jazz, hot and smooth tempos encircle the room moving up -- down -- slowly as they pick up speed, then rest

Private responses all over the room, as heads nod absorbing each note. Closed eyes signal deep thought. Feet pat to the cadence of the music, as witnessing fills the space

Musicians connect the music and each instrument rises to the occasion eagerly seizing the opportunity to let out the next note and magically know where it should be

Jazz permeates and hugs the soul

Old love

As my heart breaks, I smile

I need someone to watch over me, it plays

Fingers of the pianist tinkle a new love song, I dance the waltz of the lonely

As my old love passes by, I remember when my heart smiled

As the pianist plays a new love song, the sweetness of lost love makes me remember; I dance a waltz of remembrance

As two lovers pass, I chuckle to myself, reflect and think *why be sad*? Love is everywhere. I get another chance to find it

As the piano plays, I dance to possibilities and loneliness transcends to joy

Love is never lost; it whirls and twirls around us. DANCE the waltz of hope, splendor, and romance

As the piano plays, I celebrate me and true love

Play on piano, play on!

Music

Music all around sending sounds of gaiety, clouding misery and tears

Singers' voices give joy and overshadow the calamities of the day

Listeners sigh and take deep breaths to release heartfelt emotions

Restrictions in the world abound but musicians dare not conform

The message is clear: Move on, there is more to do with the music

Lyrics connect with each note as instruments merge and reflect the sounds of the soul

Deep within us, we all have a story of musical notes and melodies about life and love

Art

As the sculptor's hands caress and
form the clay a vision of what is beautiful
comes to mind

Each movement creates a shape of
wholesomeness and magnificence

Mysterious is the work of art, a masterpiece destined to
delight eyes and excite onlookers

The sculptor's hands move fluidly to capture what is in the
mind's eye and the artwork blossoms into unquestionable
beauty

And the desire of many to gaze increases

Eyes shut, the artist's hands shape and mold the clay

Finishes the sculpture

Flawless, who is she?

No need to search - she is wife, mother,
teacher, friend, lover and righteous

His Beautiful Woman!

Not Just Jazz

Soundness wrapped in music called jazz!

The flute soothes with its low, light and airy sound of each note; it warms me, and my day is no longer dreary

Sounds from a saxophone caress my body in your absence and offers me temporary healing for the here and now, that's jazz!

As the hands of the jazz pianist works the keyboard, up and down, my hands join in, strumming out love notes that say **rescue me** and loneliness go away; softly it descends with the hitting of every key, that's jazz!

Shaking off the dust of lost love, drums and cymbals join in every beat, shouting **cry no more, get over it,** healing from heartbreak is just around the corner, your tears ascend to heaven where every cry is heard, celebrate joy – it's coming your way!

Pull it together, like the bass does for the band; groove and sway to the sound of the music called jazz. If you don't know it, lay back and listen; it is where tales of love exist, healing, tears flow, memories are made, and things become just right

Jazz transforms, deep thoughts arise, as it pulls from its roots of blues, ragtime and African culture

Its beauty offers tranquil peace, expands the mind to areas of righteousness and truth. Straightening knots of anger in the brain, it transforms

A healing music for many, listen as it speaks to you in musical notes that travel the room, imprinting words, and musical expressions of peaceful enjoyment

Soundness, that's jazz!

I Dance

Dance as the words bellow from the song in my heart

It is silent to many

Tempo changes take place, but my steps keep up, fingers pop, and I can't stop dancing…every part of my body feels the melody

Don't you feel the music? I can't stop dancing

Where is it coming from? Deep within pushing up notes from songs of love, happiness, and celebration

My eyes close as emotion overtakes me

The beat picks up and I lose control

Don't you hear the music? This must be love

I like this dance

I pray the music never stops

Cool Jazz

Jazz flows like the veins in a leaf nourishing the soul with infectious rhythms

Its unstoppable force sends you into deep thought, mediation, and sheer joy

Jazz notes smile, rejoice and inspire; hear them, as they penetrate heart and soul

The earthly groove takes on shapes of jazz past and present: Dizzy, Miles

It is electrifying and cries out with style, as a trumpet, piano, and bass join forces

Misunderstood and embraced

Musicians let loose mellow harmonies, improvising elements of each note to meet the challenge

Explosion of sounds travel through the airwaves and nurture the soul, reminding us, it is jazz

Friendship

Music fills empty places in our hearts but not like a good friend

A friend's laughter hits the right key, and it becomes a contagious celebration

Hugs of a friend squeeze away sorrow and releases it into the air until it becomes like the sound of good music

A friend's listening ear deafens the noise of sadness and comforts our hearts

Friendship stirs the soul to dance with joy, keeps us smiling and starts us singing a melody of merriment

The music of friendship is an everlasting memory and very special in our hearts because it fills all empty places

Emptiness (Hearts Beating Without Purpose)

Music fills the hollow hole of silence

Empty words are like clouds that dissipate and vanish into the air, voiding the feelings of others

An empty heart turns away love, settling for the philosophy of self and I, like music with just one repeating note of me, me, me

Vision synced on one track, missing hearts crying out to touch, love, and sing sweet melodies that make the heart flutter

Joy, peace, and love call out and knock to enter, blocked by the wall of fear shielding emptiness

Open hands of persistence with bracelets of kindness and music of understanding hover with hope to fill the emptiness with fullness of life, music of purpose and substance

Shed your emptiness and embrace your gifts

Celebrate purpose, celebrate life

ACKNOWLEDGEMENTS

Praising and honoring God for the gifts and talents of storytelling and for the vision to write this book of poems. There are so many that have supported my journey – too many to list – but know that I am forever grateful for your belief in my worth and for your consistent encouragement. You have been there for me, giving your raw opinions on my writings, which I absolutely loved and humbly accepted with much gratitude. I appreciate all you have done to help me push past my procrastination of publishing these poems that many of you have inspired me to write. Our moments of being together bring me joy as we walk the friendship paths of joy, pain, love, and celebration.

May God bless you always.

About Jacklyn Ireland

What started me on the road to writing poems were stories told by friends and relatives, experiences, and jazz music, which I have continually enjoyed throughout my life. Hearing a single word or two triggered thoughts or viewing an object that caught my eye -- all these interactions would start my brain to generate a poem. Also, the Holy Spirit would help me along the way when I'd get stuck on making my words make sense, which happened often.

The world would call me a poet; however, I am just a sharer of words that create thoughts, confusion for some, and beauty for others. I started writing poems later in life.

I was on track to work in child development. I worked with children for a few years and loved it; however, a tragedy in my life caused me to change direction, and I ended up in the corporate and nonprofit sector for many years. Life changes happen, but I loved reading and sharing books, nursery rhymes, poems and storytelling with children, which I continue to do at children's parties. A love of poetry really increased as I studied the literary and writing module within my communications studies while pursuing a second degree.

This is my debut book of poems which explores the poetry of love, nature, spirituality, and music that influences lives.

Jacklyn Ireland is a faith-filled, vivacious senior who is a jewelry designer, loves to travel, listens to jazz, serves in her church and community, and believes in living life to the fullest.

www.ingramcontent.com/pod-product-compliance
Lightning Source LLC
Chambersburg PA
CBHW030044100526
44590CB00011B/328